All About

Ryan Reynolds

Ryan Reynolds Biography Children's Book for Kids

(With Bonus! Coloring Pages and Videos)

By All About Book

Before You Go Any Further, Get Your FREE Gift! (Worth $67)

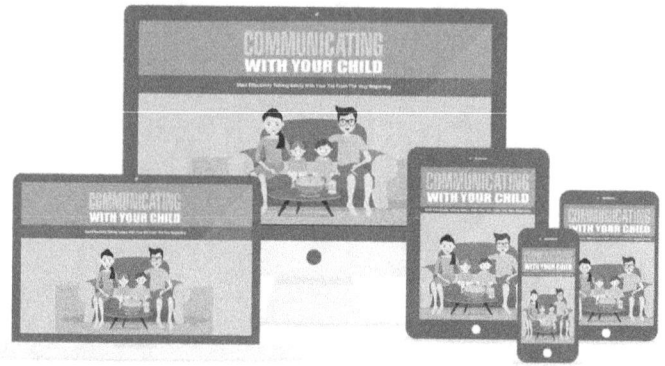

Never Fear "The Call" from the School or the Hospital Again!
How to Effectively Communicate With Your Child About *Safety* in a <u>Fun Way!</u>

Did you know if children are not taught properly about safety at a young age, it can potentially lead to reckless, dangerous behaviors even when they become a teenager or an adult?

Never fear "the call" from the school or the hospital with this comprehensive video course!

It'll teach you how to communicate effectively with your young ones about safety without boring them!

(Limited-Time FREE Gift)
Get It Before It Expires Here:

https://allaboutbookseries.com/freegift/

Table of Contents

Disclaimer and Note to Readers:

This book is an unofficial tribute book to Ryan Reynolds from a fan to support his legacy.

The information in this book is provided for educational and entertainment purposes only.

The information in this book has been compiled from reliable sources. It is accurate to the best of the author's knowledge; however, the author cannot guarantee its accuracy and validity and cannot be held liable for any errors or omissions.

If you use the information contained in this book, you agree that the author is free from and not liable for any damages, costs, and expenses, including any legal fees, potentially resulting from applying any of the information provided by this guide.

The disclaimer applies to any damages or injury caused by the use and application, whether directly or indirectly, of any advice or information presented, whether for breach of contract, tort, neglect, personal injury, criminal intent, or under any other cause of action. You agree to accept all risks of using the information presented inside this book.

If an individual cites this publication as the source of information, it does not imply that the author or publisher endorse the individual or organization's knowledge. This book is an unofficial fan tribute and has not been approved or endorsed by Ryan Reynolds or his associates.

Introduction to Ryan Reynolds

The first thing that comes to mind when Ryan Reynolds is mentioned is *Deadpool*, his funny jokes, his relationship with his wife, Blake Lively, and how they often roast each other on social media.

Ryan Reynolds was born in Canada. He's an American actor, comedian, and businessman. Ryan Reynolds just seems like the average American boy next door. However, there is so much more to him than just being the average funny guy or even *Deadpool*.

He has spent up to thirty years in the entertainment industry. He has received a series of awards, including a Critics' Choice Movie Award, People's Choice Awards, a Grammy and Golden Globe nomination, and a star on the Hollywood Walk of Fame.

He is one of the highest-grossing film actors of all time, and his box-office gross is at $5 million worldwide.

The entertainer has been married twice, and he has three daughters.

From Ryan Reynolds, we have learned that giving up is not an option, and hard work and smart work are valuable. Also, consistency pays.

Biography of Ryan Reynolds

http://allaboutbookseries.com/RyanReynoldsBiography

Ryan Reynolds' Early Childhood

Ryan Rodney Reynolds arrived into the world on October 23, 1976, as the youngest of four sons in Vancouver, British Columbia, Canada. His father, James Chester Reynolds, was a royal mounted policeman before he retired and went to work as a wholesaler. Being a policeman left its mark on James. He was very strict, and his children were scared of him. His mother, Tamara Lee, worked as a cashier at a supermarket. He has three brothers: Terry, Jeff, and Patrick.

Today, he speaks about his parents with warmth.

"Now, I'm amazed at how my parents coped with four boys. How much wisdom and patience they needed. Of course, they were not perfect. But if I grew up in an ideal family, then most likely I didn't develop such a sense of humor, which is an excellent protection against the troubles of life."

He has Irish and Scottish ancestry.

Growing up, Ryan used his sense of humor as a coping mechanism. He often laughed at himself and with others. He gave himself no opportunity to get upset at others.

"I was growing up as a serious, sensitive child, strained as a bare wire. With my skin, I felt the mood, the experiences of other people. Maybe this helped me master the acting profession."

Ryan started acting at the age of thirteen. He was in high school, and he realized that he loved acting. His father was not in full support.

Question to Ponder: Have you ever been in a position where your parents didn't support something you liked?

Ryan was not deterred. He channelled his energy into sports and started playing football and baseball. He was a valuable player who was good at his craft. Sports was not his ambition, but he excelled at it in order to get the approval of his father.

Question to Ponder: Have you ever done something you didn't care about to get your parent's approval? How did it feel?

His father was delighted, so he went to all of Ryan's games, no matter the weather. At the same time, Ryan was putting himself under significant pressure. He destroyed his health by running after a ball across the field and suffering a concussion.

Early Career

Ryan Reynolds commenced acting early. His career started in 1991 when he got the role of Billy Simpson in a Canadian teen drama titled *Hillside*.

The drama was distributed in America by Nickelodeon and titled *Fifteen*. The drama showed the life of students from Hillside high school. It tackled different issues such as dating, infidelity, divorce, friendship, and alcohol abuse. Ryan Reynolds later admitted that he disliked the work. But for a younger Ryan Reynolds, the movie was perfect. He even persuaded his parents to take him for the casting because he was so into acting. He earned $150 per episode, and he felt rich. He even won the Best Young Actor on Cable TV Award. Being part of the movie made Ryan decide on his future profession.

Ryan Reynolds on Daytime TV Fifteen, 1990

http://allaboutbookseries.com/Fifteen1990

Question to Ponder: Have you ever persistently asked for something you wanted? How did it feel when you finally got it? How do you think Ryan Reynolds felt after he got the role on *Hillside*?

At the age of seventeen, he played the role of Ganesh in *Ordinary Magic*, an Indian who relocated to Canada from India after the death of his father.

Between 1993 and 1994, he played the role of Marco in *The Odyssey*; it was a recurring role.

After his role in *The Odyssey*, he went on a film hiatus. Not by choice. He graduated from secondary school and gained admission into a polytechnic school. His parents had no money, so Ryan worked as a salesman in a grocery store and as a bartender in a nightclub.

Things were not going as he expected, so he dropped out and decided to chase his dreams in Los Angeles.

Question to Ponder: Have you ever quit doing something you loved because you were not getting the desired results?

Los Angeles was not as easy as Ryan imagined. He has expressed that his early days in Los Angeles, California was difficult. The day after he moved to Los Angeles, his jeep was snatched. That was hard for him. He had to learn how to navigate the complex public transport system of Los Angeles.

Not only was his Jeep stolen, but he also was not getting roles. His failure clung to him like a turtle neck shirt, and it was taking a toll on his self-esteem.

Around that time, he met Chris William Martin, who convinced him to start acting again.

He joined a small improv comedy group known as the Grounding. Ryan mentioned that the Canadian in him made sure everyone had the spotlight on the show. Then his director spoke to him and told him to take the stage. The director told him to seize his moment, that everyone was going to have theirs, so he should stop apologizing for outlining anybody. Ryan listened to that advice, and it changed his life. It made him a stronger actor.

He started getting small roles. He starred as Jay "Boom" DeBoom in the third season of *The X-Files*.

Ryan Reynolds on The X-Files

http://allaboutbookseries.com/OnXFiles

He kept searching for jobs with Chris Martin, which led to Ryan's role in *My Name is Kate*. The plot talks about the life of an alcoholic who is trying to deal with her illness while making her family happy. Ryan plays the role of Kevin, her teenage son, who is very understanding.

It was almost impossible not to notice Ryan in that movie. One could not miss his charismatic acting and his Hollywood smile. The roles kept flowing after this.

He played the role of Griffin in *Lonesome Dove*. His role in a short episode was perfectly played. The series was about living in the wild west.

However, the series lasted one season.

Ryan didn't have time to be upset about it. He was expected on the set of a new movie, *Serving in Silence*. He had a minor role here, but he was proud of the movie as it was nominated for different awards, including an Emmy and a Golden Globe.

The following year, he also appeared in *Sabrina the Teenage Witch*; he co-starred alongside Melissa Joan Hart in 1996.

This series opened up a new realm for Ryan Reynolds when it came to movies. He played the role of Seth, a popular student and a subject of admiration for the female student body. Sabrina was also trying to fall in love with him. Classic.

In the series, he showed his excellent sense of humor. That led to a turning point for him. He started getting comedic roles.

He also appeared in *Cold Blood*, the miniseries adapted from Truman Capote's book, *Cold Blood*. He played the role of Bobby Rupp, the boyfriend of a murdered teenage girl. This role helped him break out of the classic handsome guy in family films for a short while.

He then starred in *When Friendship Kills*. The film talks about bulimia. Ryan plays the role of the handsome guy with whom the main character is in love.

Then he stars in *The Outer Limits* as Paul. While the film lasted for seven years, Ryan's character didn't.

It is essential to note that most of Ryan's Roles were similar. He played the handsome boy. He spent time auditioning for roles after roles just to get more serious roles, but the handsome boy roles clung to him. However, his distinct sense of humor set him apart from other actors who were often given the handsome boy role.

In 1997, Ryan played Howard in the comedy *Life during Wartime*. The cast of this movie were real movie stars. Ryan had the opportunity to learn from them. He had a real comedic role, and he thrived in his role. The film was witty.

In 1998, he played the role of medical student Michael Bergen in *Two Guys, a Girl, and a Pizza Place*. The film tells the story of three flatmates and a pizza place: Beacon Street Pizza. Berg worked in the pizza place with Pete, his flatmate. The major part of the four seasons focuses on Pete and Berg's relationship and how they relate with Sharon, who lives in the apartment above them. It was hilarious and well-received.

Ryan starred in three more films while filming the series. He was in *Dick*, where he played the role of Chip Halderman, the son of Halderman, the White House Chief of Staff. He was fooled by Betsy so that Arlene could sneak into the Chief of Staff's house. He had just about five minutes of screen time, but he still stole the show.

He also played the role of Henry Rockefeller Lipschitz, a garage band musician in *Coming Soon*. He later becomes the boyfriend of Stream, one of the main characters.

The Early 2000s

In 2000, he starred as the undead in *Big Monster on Campus*, and he was in *We All Fall Down*. Then he played the role of Mike in *Buying the Cow*. The film was about how difficult people find it to part with a bachelor's life. Mike was the best friend of David, the main character. Mike thought he was gay because he thought he had slept with a man. He made numerous awkward attempts to come out of the closet.

After his role in *Buying the Cow*, the director recognized his charismatic personality, as well as his clear facial expression when interpreting roles, so he decided to cast Ryan in his new project, *National Lampoon's Van Wilder*. He worked with Tara Reid and Kal Penn; their work was successful. It resulted in $40 million at the box office. Ryan Reynolds was cast as the title character *Van Wilder*. The plot of the film talks about the misadventures of Van wilder.

Van Wilder has gone through college as a party animal. His mission is to help undergraduates succeed in college. Soon an article written by Gwen goes out about his party lifestyle. This gets the attention of his father. As a result, his father cuts his tuition. Now Van, while struggling to graduate, must find a way to pay his tuition. Somehow, he finds himself in a love triangle with Gwen and her boyfriend, Richard, who continuously sabotages Van. When Van throws a party, Richard brings in underage children and calls the police. Van is arrested for providing alcohol to minors and facing possible expulsion. His friend Taj convinces him to fight the charges. Van does and tells the court to force him to graduate. He is forced to sit for exams that begin in six days. Van passes the exams and finally graduates. A party is thrown to celebrate his achievements. Ryan's acting was flawless, and he received praises for the role. He was nominated for an MTV movie award for this role. Also, this film opened more acting opportunities for him.

The succeeding years were filled with Ryan playing comic roles. He was cast in the comedy series *scrubs*. He played the role of Spence, the former college classmate of the main characters: JD and Turks. He appeared in just one episode. He also revealed that Jordan's baby was also Dr. Cox's baby.

He also appeared in *The In-Laws* with Michael Douglas. He played the role of Mark Tobias, the son of Steve Tobias, an undercover CIA agent played by Michael Douglas. The film is an action-comedy that follows Steve Tobias and Jerry Peyser. Peyser stumbles on Tobias' secret, which is to set up an arms deal so they can catch arms smugglers. While Jerry doesn't want to be part of the mission, he gets involved either coincidentally or by trickery. While the film itself was funny, it failed at the box office as it just got $27 million of the $40 million budgeted for it.

2003 came with more roles for Ryan Reynolds. He also played Kevin in *FoolProof* that year. He starred with David Suchet. The film is about a group of friends who jokingly plan grand heists as a game but never carry them out. Things turn when someone breaks into their house, steals the plan, and successfully carries it out. The criminal, Leo, blackmails them into planning and executing a heist. He threatens to go to the authorities with the plan if they don't.

So the friends help him plan how he can steal $20 million in bonds from a bank. The heist goes in Leo's favor as he assumes he killed the friends. Meanwhile, they switch his gun, giving him one with blanks. The friends burn his house to destroy the evidence he had on them and plant proof of the new heist on him. He is then arrested, and the friends drive off.

He was cast in *Harold & Kumar Go to White Castle* with Neil Patrick Harris, John Cho, and Kal Penn. He acted as an OR nurse in the hospital where Kumar's brother and father work.

He also received the Hollywood award for being a promising young actor.

In 2004, filmmaker David Goyer decided that Ryan Reynolds would be great on the cast of *Blade*. So he was cast on *Blade: Trinity*, the final movie of the *Blade* trilogy, alongside Wesley Snipes. He played the role of the Hannibal King, a former vampire who is now a member of the vampire hunting group Nightstalker. The character was created based on the Hannibal King of the Blade comic.

In this instalment, Blade gets framed for murders by the vampires. They have joined forces with the FBI to locate Blade and bring him to them (the vampires.) The FBI finds him, but Hannibal King and Abigail Whistler rescue him. He is invited to help them hunt vampires. He discovers that Danica Talos had revived Dracula, or Drake, as he is known.

Drake plans to wipe the earth of vampires and humans as he sees them as inferior beings. The vampires plan for human subjugation. The Nightstalkers plan to kill Drake genetically and, by extension, other vampires by unleashing a virus.

At the end of the movie, Drake and Blade fight; Drake bests Blade, but he's shot by an arrow that has the virus. It mixes with his blood and becomes airborne, killing the other vampires. Drake also insinuates that Blade is the future of the vampiric race.

To fit into the role, he had to gain ten kilograms of muscle mass. He also had to learn martial arts. He has mentioned that the training was brutal. *Blade: Trinity* was Ryan's first-ever Marvel film. His performance reminded one of the crew members of *Deadpool*.

The actor has revealed that filming *Blade* was rugged. Wesley Snipes is a method actor, and it was difficult to break him out of character. He often tried to break Snipes out of character, but he failed. He had to improvise many of his lines to make it fun. He, along with other cast members, would think of the worst jokes to say to Snipes but would never get a reaction.

In a recent interview, Reynolds revealed that he never met Snipes. The person he met was Blade.

Ryan Reynolds in 2005-2009

2005 started well for Ryan Reynolds. He began to get more serious roles after the success of *Blade: Trinity*.

Amityville Horror

In 2005, after *Blade*, Ryan decided to try new genres. His characters and storylines got deeper. He played George Lutz, the lead character in *Amityville*, the horror remake in 2005. Lutz moved to a new house with his wife Kathy and her kids from a previous marriage. The home is located in Amityville, New York. The new house is gorgeous, and judging from the deal they got from the place, it's too good to be true. The former resident of that house murdered his family after the devil possessed him. George Lutz is losing it, and he must find a priest to send out the devil from the house.

Talking about the character, Ryan mentioned that his meltdown was intriguing. The unravelling of his on-screen character also affected him badly. He slapped his on-screen child, though it was not part of the script.

While filming the movie, he stayed away from his step kids. He didn't want to know them and get attached to them because it would affect his role in the film. It worked perfectly. He also mentioned that the children were okay with it. He took his part in *Amityville* seriously, and he was okay with the result.

School of Life

He was also in the *School of Life*. He played the role of Mr. D, the new students' favorite. The plot reveals two opposing teachers, Mr. D and Matt Warner, who compete for the title of Teacher of the Year. Matt Warner, whose father won Teacher of the Year, has pressured himself to follow in his father's footsteps. Realizing he's not the students' favorite, he's trying hard to discredit Mr. D. He keeps digging for anything he can use against Mr. D. Soon, he finds out that Mr. D has lung cancer and does not have long to live. He realizes that in his pettiness, he has not been a good teacher, so he changes his ways. Mr. D wins the Teacher of the Year, but he dies that year.

Just Friends

He also got the lead role of Chris in *Just Friends*. The film tells the story of Chris Brander. As a high school senior, he was obese and in love with his best friend, Jamie. He confesses it in her yearbook. Jamie's boyfriend reads it out loud to everyone, humiliating Chris. Jamie kisses his cheeks and tells him that his feelings are not mutual. He leaves, swearing never to come back and be more successful than others.

Ten years later, he is a famous record producer and the Vice President of his company. Just before Christmas, he is asked by the company's CEO to accompany Samantha, a singer, to Paris. The label is interested in signing her. Samantha wants a relationship with Chris, but he's not interested as their previous date landed him in the hospital.

Fate has other plans for Chris. On their way to Paris, Samantha sets her private jet on fire by mistake. This causes them to crash land beside Chris' hometown. He takes Samantha to his childhood home, where they meet his mother and brother. His brother is a big fan of Samantha, so he's excited to see her.

He finds out that Jamie works as a bartender in the local pub so that she can afford graduate school. Chris and Jamie go on an ice skating date. There he injures himself as a result of a hockey game gone wrong. The paramedics pick up Chris, and Jamie is reunited with Dusty, a former classmate.

When Chris decides to confess his love to Jamie, he finds Dusty at her house, impressing everyone with a guitar. Samantha finds his whereabouts after bribing his brother with a kiss. She drives to Jamie's house and destroys the Christmas decorations. Chris is embarrassed and keeps apologizing. Jamie tells him she's not offended.

Chris visits a friend for advice and then overhears Dusty telling a nurse that he has plans to humiliate Jamie. Chris tries to warn Jamie about Dusty, which turns into a big fight.

He returns home and keeps rejecting Samantha's advances. He soon realizes that Jamie is the love of his life, so he goes back, apologizes, and confesses his love, and they kiss.

The film grossed a total of $50.9 million. In reviews, it got both good and bad reviews.

Waiting

He also appeared as Monty Cook, the roommate and friend of the main character, Dean, in the film *Waiting*. Monty is also the head cook of the restaurant. He is also a morally corrupt man who likes underage girls. Ryan acted his character well. The movie earned US $6 million on its opening weekend. This is more than double its budget.

Smokin' Aces

He also played the role of Richard Menser, an FBI agent in *Smokin' Aces* in 2006. He starred with Ben Affleck, Alicia Keys, Jason Bateman, and Taraji P. Henson in the movie. There is a bounty worth a million dollars on daytime Las Vegas magician and gangster wannabe Israel, who is also known as "Aces." Many people want the bounty, so they are out to get Israel. Reynold's role is to protect Israel and ensure his testimony.

Ryan played three characters in the psychological thriller *The Nines*. He played the role of Gary, an actor under house arrest. He lives in the house of a TV writer who is away at work because he burned his house. He makes friends with Margaret, a PR handler, and Sarah, the next-door single mom. During his house arrest, he keeps seeing the number nine and thinks he's being haunted by the number nine. He breaks the green anklet he's been wearing during his house arrest, which damages reality.

In the second part of the film, Ryan plays the role of Gavin, a TV writer who is trying to get his TV show titled "Knowing" produced. The show is about a single mother and her daughter who are lost. The TV show stars his friend Melissa as the main character. While the show is being reviewed, Susan, a TV producer, tells him to look for the nines. He writes it on paper, which Gary found in the first part. During the post-production process, Susan convinces him to drop Melissa for a different famous actress. It leads to an argument, but he does it. He contacts the other actress and discovers she can't do his project because she's tied down with another project. Angrily he confronts Susan, complaining that she led him on even though she knew his project would never be picked up. The argument gets more heated, he slaps her, and she insults his masculinity.

When he gets out, he sees sevens floating but somehow, a nine is floating on him. He remembers what Margaret, his PR handler, told him of how humans are seven, koalas are eights, and nines are gods, and they exist in different forms. Gavin does not believe this. This is revealed to be the reason why Gary escaped from house arrest.

The third part of the film features Ryan playing the role of Gabriel, a video game designer. His car breaks down in the middle of the road with his daughter Noelle and wife Mary. He leaves them in a bid to get service on his phone. He gets picked up by a woman named Sierra, who gives him a ride to the gas station. Meanwhile, his daughter sees a video of Gary and Margaret in part one and Gavin and Melissa in part two. She shows her mom, who is confused about it.

Gabriel becomes ill because Sierra drugged his water. In all the stories, Sierra, Susan, and Sarah were trying to get Gavin Gabriel and Gary from Mary, Melissa, and Margaret because that life was not a reality. She informs him that he is God and he has made himself into different reincarnations for four thousand years, and now he is needed at home. She explained it using Gabriel's love for video games. He returned home, and the film ended with Melissa married to Ben and Noelle as their daughter.

The film was well-received, and it even received a nomination for best DVD at the 34th Saturn Awards.

In 2008, he played the role of Frank Allen in *Chaos Theory*. Frank Allen liked to live his life based on a schedule. He strictly followed the time. However, his wife, Susan, playfully turns the clock back by ten minutes so he can run an errand for her one morning when he has to deliver a life-changing lecture. This spurs a series of chaotic events. First, he misses his ferry, then arrives late for his time management lecture. This seems significant, but it is the least of the chaos the universe has planned.

On his way home, he meets a pregnant woman in need of help. He takes her to the hospital, saving her life. At the hospital, he fills in his details for the pregnant woman. Before he arrives home, a nurse at the hospital calls his home, attempting to reach the baby's father. His wife believes that he has cheated on her, so she throws his things out of the house. Frank tries to explain, but she refuses to listen. Trying to find proof that he's not the baby's daddy, he discovers that he cannot have children. So who is the father of his daughter? The whole situation is complex as Frank finds out his wife has been cheating on him.

His wife later finds out the truth, but it looks like it's late. He starts living his life randomly and without a schedule. He later finds out that his friend is the biological father of his daughter. Hurt, he wants to harm his friend; but the friend saves his life. He realizes he still loves his wife and daughter, so he returns home.

The character of Frank is such a deep one as he has a difficult decision to make.

In 2008, Ryan starred in *Definitely Maybe* as Will Hayes, a former political consultant who now works at an advertising firm. The movie navigates how he helps his ten-year-old daughter understand his approaching divorce from her mother. He tells how he met her mother, changing some of the names.

After graduating from university, Will leaves his college sweetheart Emily and moves to New York City. He is to deliver a package to Emily's friend. It contains a diary which he reads and discovers some interesting things about Emily.

He later meets April, a colleague, and they become close. He informs her of his plans to propose to Emily. They visit April's apartment, and Will notices her many copies of *Jane Eyre*. She tells him that her dad gave her a copy of the book with a personal inscription, but it was lost, so she spends time buying second-hand books with notes.

Emily visits, and when Will tries to propose to her, she tells him to move on and confesses that she had betrayed his trust with his former co-worker.

April leaves, and he meets Summer. He likes her, and he's about to propose to her. But he discovers that she has written an article that could ruin his career. He tries to talk her out of publishing it, but she refuses. Will ends their relationship, and his career suffers as a result of the article.

Years later, he is reunited with April, who throws a party to bring him out of his depression. He tells her he loves her, which leads to an argument. He leaves and actually finds the copy of *Jane Eyre* that her father left her. He goes to give it but decides against it when he finds out that she is living with her boyfriend.

He runs into Summer, who invites him to a party after telling him she's pregnant. He reconnects with Emily at the party.

His daughter deduces that Emily is her mother.

While he tells her the story, his daughter wishes that her parents would come back together, but the divorce is finalized. Will assures his daughter that she is the happy ending.

After the divorce, he moves to a new environment where he finds out he is lonely without April, the love of his life. Also, he doesn't change her name while telling the story. With his daughter urging and supporting him, he visits April and confesses that he loves her. The two of them share a kiss.

In 2009, Ryan Reynolds played the role of Wade Wilson in *X-Men Origins*, the prequel of the X-Men films. While he was filming *Blade*, there had been some discussions about Ryan playing Deadpool if it was ever adapted into a movie. He even told filmmaker David Goyer that he was interested in playing the character.

Ryan Reynolds on X-Men Origins

http://allaboutbookseries.com/XMenOrigins

So when the opportunity came to play the character, Ryan was considered.

However, this version of *Deadpool* was not what Ryan had in mind when he wanted to play Deadpool. Ryan expressed that before he accepted the role; he mentioned to the producers that it was the wrong version of Deadpool

This version has no personality, and his mouth was sewn shut. They literally took the nickname "merc with a mouth" the other way.

Ryan mentioned that when the filming happened, it was during the writer's strike of 2007. So when it came to the lines, he was on his own. Most of the lines of Wade Wilson, also known as Deadpool, were written by him. He also mentioned that he had fun at the beginning of production, but they switched up things in the later part of production and not in a good way.

Question to Ponder: How would you feel if someone recreates the image of your favorite superhero?

2008 had Ryan, the sweetheart of romantic comedies, getting married. He married Scarlett Johansson. The marriage lasted two years. There have been different speculations about why they split. The most common one was that Ryan could not handle a successful woman. The rumors did not bother Ryan; he focused on his career and kept doing better.

Adventureland

Ryan Reynolds also played the role of Mike Connell, the maintenance man of the park. He has a wife named Ronnie. He is a part-time musician who claims to have played with Lou Reed. However, that is not the case. He does not have much knowledge about music. Also, he's having an affair with Emily Lewin, one of the workers of Adventureland Park. She is also the love interest of James, the main character in the film. Soon, the affair between Mike and Emily starts to spread when one of James' co-workers tells him about it. He later sees Em leaving Mike's house. Then he tells a co-worker, and the news becomes public. Em leaves the park. James and Em later reconcile and date. The film got positive reviews, and it earned more than its budget at the box office.

Paper Man

This film is also referred to as *Unlikely Hero*. The plot of the film follows the friendship between two different people. Richard is a struggling hero with an imaginary friend, while Abby is a teenage girl with an imaginary friend. In this film, Ryan Reynolds plays the role of Captain Excellent, Richard's imaginary friend. Captain Excellent tells Richard that he can never make a good decision without his help. Also, about his friendship with Abby, Captain Excellent tells Richard that the friendship can only lead to bad things. At the end of the film, Richard bids goodbye to his imaginary friend as it's time for him to navigate life on his own. The film got negative reception.

Question to Ponder: How do you think Ryan felt about this film?

He also starred in the romantic movie *The Proposal* with Sandra Bullock and Betty White. The movie is about Margaret Tate, a Canadian immigrant in the US. She is disliked by everyone who works with her. Ryan Reynolds plays the role of Andrew, her assistant, who is blackmailed into marrying her after she finds out that her visa will not be renewed due to visa terms violation. The immigration agent informs them that he suspects that they are committing fraud so Margaret can get her visa. He warns them that if they commit fraud, Margaret will be deported, and Andrew will face a jail term of five years and a fine of $250,000.

Andrew tells Margaret to promote him to the editor immediately after the wedding and publish the book he has been suggesting.

Then they travel to Alaska, Andrew's hometown. There Margaret finds out that Andrew's family is wealthy. She also discovers that he is close with his family and confesses that she has forgotten what it feels like to belong in a family. She reveals their deal, the immigration agent is there, and he informs her that she has 24 hours to leave the country. She leaves. When Andrew realizes that she has left, he thinks about going after her. His grandmother has a heart attack, and they were airlifted. Grammy confesses that she faked the heart attack and urges Ryan to go after Margaret. They reunite and get married for real this time.

Ryan Reynolds' Career from 2010

The new decade comes with Ryan getting even more serious roles.

Buried

He was cast in *Buried* as Paul Conroy, an American truck driver based in Iraq. In the film, Paul is attacked, then he finds himself in a wooden coffin with a lighter, his blackberry, and a pen. In the dark, he takes us back to what happened to him and how he got there. He calls the Ohio cops and the FBI, but they don't help. He is then called by his kidnapper to pay $5 million, make a video, or he would be left to die in the coffin.

He called the state department, and they informed him that the government has a policy of not negotiating with terrorists, but they would try to save him. He is told not to make the video, but he makes it after his kidnappers threaten his co-worker. The video is viral, and the state Department is livid. They terminate his employment, and he is told that if he does, his family will not be entitled to any benefits. He communicates with his family, and he finds out they are okay. There were attempts to save him; unfortunately, he suffocates after he wills his properties to his family.

The film revealed his dramatic flair. It received mixed reactions from critics. Some called it a masterpiece like no other. It was a challenging role as Ryan returned to Los Angeles with scratches on his back. Rodrigo Cortez, the film director, mentioned that Ryan never complained about anything during the shooting, not even the sand. "We poured tons of sand on him, and it was not just sand that scratched and peeled off the skin. It was mixed with dust. Ryan breathed dust. It clogged his eyes too. It was very difficult for him because this is a difficult role."

He was nominated for several awards for this role, including the MTV awards, IGN Movie Award for Best Performance, and GOYA awards. He also won the Saturn Award for Best Actor.

However, he developed insomnia and post-traumatic stress disorder because of the role. He got used to the role; it affected his everyday life. "Every night, I couldn't fall asleep... I returned home feeling that I was suffering from some strange form of PTSD if, of course, this applies to filmmaking. In short, I couldn't get myself together. It was really difficult. After Barcelona, I could not come to my senses for some time."

In 2011, Ryan played the role of Green Lantern. It was a temporary switch from Marvel Cinematic University to DC. This was because Ryan felt that Green Lantern would make a fine superhero. However, he regretted making the movie. The movie was said to be a high-profile failure. Ryan was not the first choice to play the superhero, so, as a result, there was a clash on set. The investors, in a bid to make profits, kept interfering with the movie process. There were a lot of studio effects. Honestly, the whole production was a mess. Some reports say that the studio took the film from the director and finished editing without his input.

That's not to say that people didn't work hard to make the movie a success, but it flopped.

Ryan Reynolds Watches Green Lantern The First Time

http://allaboutbookseries.com/GreenLantern

Question to Ponder: Have you ever worked hard at something, and it didn't come out well? How do you think Ryan felt about the Green Lantern film?

While the movie was a flop, something good came out of the filming—his relationship with Blake Lively. The duo was a couple on screen, and after the film was released, they became a real-life couple. They got married in 2012 and are still married today. The actor's secret to a happy home is, "Don't forget to be friends and always make fun of each other." The couple's social media account testifies to their making fun of each other. It is always fun to watch.

He also did a voice-over for *Family Guy* in which he played himself.

He still acted in comedies.

The Change-Up

He was cast in *The Change-Up* as Mitch Planko. The film portrays how a family man changed places with a bachelor. The plot follows two best friends, Mitch and Dave, who urinate in a fountain while simultaneously wishing for each other's life. Their bodies get switched. The following day, they return to get their bodies back, but the fountain is nowhere to be found. It turns out that it has been moved for restoration. Forced to wait till the fountain is located, they decide to live each other's lives.

As it turns out, living as someone else is difficult. Mitch, while living Dave's life, sabotages a merger with a firm. Dave, while living Mitch's life, shoots an X-rated film.

When it's time to switch bodies, things get out of hand. They are chased by the park security but manage to escape. Living in each other's bodies made them develop a new level of respect for each other. It did well at the box office, but it received a lot of criticism.

He also played the role of Matt Weston in *Safehouse*. The film features Matt, a low-level CIA agent who guards a safe house in Cape Town for the agency. The agency is investigating Tobin Frost, a former agent who allegedly betrayed the agency. Denzel Washington plays Frost. The safe house is attacked, with most agents dying, while Matt escapes with Frost. The enemies seem to be almost one step ahead of Frost and Matt. Frost starts to exploit Matt by feeding him lies. He tells him that there's someone in the agency informing the enemy of their whereabouts. He also tells Matt that he will be forced to take the fall if things go wrong. He gives his girlfriend an excuse to make if the CIA interviews her. Matt starts to fear for his life when his boss tells him, "We'll take it from here" after Frost escapes. Frost had earlier warned him about that phrase. Matt decided to find Frost on his own.

Matt finds Frost and helps him escape from the enemy. After interrogating one of the mercenaries, Matt finds out they are working for the CIA. Frost advises Matt not to kill innocent people. They move to a new safe house, where the safe housekeeper injures Matt after they fight. Frost reveals that he has a file exposing corruption in the CIA. Frost gives the file to Matt, saying he is a better man than he is. Matt goes back to the United States, where he is promoted.

The film was well-received. It had a gross total of $208,076,205. This is Ryan Reynolds's sixth most significant opening of a movie.

He didn't stop there. Ryan kept doing more films.

In this film, Ryan Reynolds plays the role of Matthew Lane, a man whose daughter is kidnapped from his truck after he leaves her for a few minutes. This event spurs the whole film. When his daughter was kidnapped, he was treated as the suspect. Eight years after the incident, his daughter has not been found, and he is estranged from his wife. There seems to be evidence that his daughter is alive. And she is, except that her kidnapper is currently using her as a pawn to lure younger girls in. Matthew is tricked by his daughter's kidnapper into seeing her. He is knocked out.

When he wakes up, he later hears the kidnappers talking and follows one of them to a restaurant. He confronts them while disrupting the peace in the restaurant, which makes the restaurant call the police. He steals a phone from the kidnappers, which buys him time. The police get the kidnappers, and his family is reunited. The film had a limited release. However, it's available for streaming on Netflix.

In Ryan fashion, he still acts in comedies. He did a lot of action comedies. He acted as Nick Walker in the film *Rest in Peace Department*. It is based on a graphic novel about two cops. One of them has been dead for hundreds of years, while the other one just recently died. Their job is to try to keep the dead quiet and dead.

The film was hilarious, but it was not well received. The plot of the film follows Nick Walker, a policeman whose partner killed him after he decided that he would submit the gold he stole as evidence.

When he died, he was taken to a room in the afterlife. He was told that he was facing eternal damnation for stealing, but he could work as a police officer for penance. He is sent to the Rest in Peace Department, whose duty is to collect souls that are not ready to cross to the afterlife. They are known as deados. He is introduced to his partner, Roy, who used to be a US Marshall when he was alive. They go back to the graveyard, and they watch Nick's funeral. He tries to reach out to his wife, who does not recognize him. Roy tells him that their images have been altered so no one from their past can recognize them.

The duo begins its jobs. Their first mission is to interrogate a suspected deado who has gold similar to what Nick stole at the beginning. They get the gold and submit it as evidence. They visit one of Roy's informants, who is tricked into revealing that Nick's former partner, Hayes, was the dealer. They go to Hayes's house. They see him giving Nick's gold to a deado. They try to get the gold, but the deado transforms into a monster.

Nick and Roy are suspended from their job, but they still go after the deados. The gold that is being stolen is for them to restore the staff of Jericho. Nick's former partner Hayes and his team of deados steal all the gold and kidnap Julia, Nick's wife, to use as a human sacrifice to activate the staff. Nick kills Hayes, and the team is destroyed. His wife, whom Hayes has injured, is close enough to death to see Nick. They reconcile, and Nick tells his wife to live for them.

Talking about the film, Reynolds mentioned that he had to tweak his character to fit his personality. The film was not renewed for a second part because it did poorly at the box office.

In 2013, Ryan played the voice of different animation characters.

He was the voice of Theo, also known as Turbo, in the animation *Turbo*. He was a snail who dreamt of becoming a racer. His family members used to laugh at him.

Ryan Reynolds the Voice of Turbo

http://allaboutbookseries.com/TurboMovie

He got super speed accidentally and went on to compete and win at a car race. He was also a voice character in *The Croods*. In *The Croods*, he voiced the character of Guy, a teenage cave boy who is more evolved than others. Guy finds new intentions to make life easier for him. He also thinks with the help of his pet Sloth, Belt. Guy and Eep have romantic feelings toward each other

.

http://allaboutbookseries.com/TheCroodsInterview

In 2014, Ryan returned to the horror genre. He played the role of psychopath Jerry in *The Voices*. Jerry is a kind young man who is mentally ill. He has hallucinations that his pets could talk to him and tell him what to do. Jerry inherited his illness from his mother, who had schizophrenia. We find out that he had a troubled childhood. He started showing the symptoms of schizophrenia at a young age.

The Superhero

Growing up, Ryan read a lot of comics, and he wanted to be a superhero. He got to be Deadpool in *X-Men*, but that didn't end well. In 2015, the opportunity presented itself again. This time around, *Deadpool* was well written, and he had enough character to appeal to the audience.

Ryan Reynolds Talk About Deadpool

http://allaboutbookseries.com/DeadpoolInterview

Deadpool tells the story of a former special forces operative who turned into a mercenary. He was experimented on by rogues. This gave him fast healing abilities. He is known as Merc with a mouth because of the famous jokes he tells. He has a twisted sense of humor. He is mentally unstable. He developed an alter ego and decided to hunt down the person who ruined his life. He is an antihero. He's not the good guy or bad guy. He does what he wants.

Before he was given the role of Deadpool, Ryan wrote a lot to 20th Century Fox to fund a *Deadpool* spinoff, but they didn't answer. Also, they were skeptical about casting him after the failure of *Green Lantern*. However, he was given the role due to his persistence and support from fans. Ryan mentioned that while he had been an ambassador for the *Deadpool* film for eleven years, he didn't do much. Fans did most of the work. Someone leaked test footage of *Deadpool*; fans saw it and got mad. They kept sending hate emails demanding a *Deadpool* film.

Question to Ponder: Have you ever gotten something after persistently asking for it? How do you think Ryan felt after he got the role of Deadpool?

After he got the role, Ryan worked hard to prove that he deserved the role. First, he worked so hard in the gym that he bulked up. The lining of the dead pool suit had to be removed so he could fit in. Also, he spent a long time in the mask, and we still happened to see facial expressions.

He also got producer credit for the film. For him, it was a way of protecting Wade Wilson/Deadpool. In *X-Men*, he couldn't dictate how the character should go, but with the producer's credit, he could come out to say a particular thing was not how the character should be portrayed.

He claimed that he was annoying to be around as he knew every minute detail of Deadpool.

The film was critically acclaimed, and Ryan won MTV awards for best fighting and comedy. He didn't win a Golden Globe, but he was happy. His acting had been restored in the comic community. It is symbolic for him that it was his comic book hero that brought him real fame. Deadpool was a long-term goal for Ryan; after the film was released, he claimed to have an existential crisis. He mentioned that he had the shakes, and it felt as if he had a neurological problem. He visited different doctors after, and they diagnosed him with anxiety.

After the release of *Deadpool*, Ryan played the role of Michael in *The Hitman's Bodyguard*. He starred alongside Samuel L. Jackson. The duo was memorable. The plot of the film follows Michael Bruce, a successful bodyguard used to a luxurious lifestyle. Then his Japanese client, who is an arms dealer, is assassinated. This leads to a fall on the grass.

Two years later, Dukhovich, the dictator of Belarus, is facing trial for crimes against humanity. The Interpol decided to bring Darius Kincaid, a notorious criminal who has been imprisoned, to testify. He negotiates a deal to testify if his wife is released.

After the negotiation, he is taken to a safe house by Interpol. They are attacked by Dukhovich's men with the aid of a corrupt officer. Kincaid eliminates the attackers, but there's only one Interpol left. Agent Roussel. She calls Michael Bryce to accompany Kincaid to a new safehouse.

They begin their journey, and Kincaid reveals that he shot Bryce's Japanese client. Annoyed, Bryce abandons him. Reminiscing about his past mistakes at a bar, Bryce decides to go back to accompany Kincaid, who has been attacked by Dukhovich's men. He returns to rescue Kincaid, but he is kidnapped in the process. Kincaid rescues him, and they sort their differences.

Kincaid testifies against Dukhovich, who admits guilt. He bombed the court and then tried to kill Kincaid. Bryce dives in, taking the bullet for Kincaid. He then kills the snitch in the Interpol. Kincaid kills Dukovhich but is re-arrested for his crimes. He later breaks out of jail to meet his wife.

Ryan Reynolds did another horror film in 2017. Starring opposite Jake Gyllenhaal and Rebecca Ferguson in the film *Life*, he played his role well. In this film, scientists discover the first evidence of life on Mars. The International space station takes a dormant cell sample from it. It grows into a multi-celled organism named Calvin. The scientists in the lab discover that Calvin's cells can change a lot about humans. So, they start experimenting. One day during the experimentation process, it becomes hostile, escapes, and swallows a lab rat. He becomes more extensive and tries to attack the engineer. Rory Adams saves him, but Calvin holds on to his leg, so Adams is locked in with Calvin, who devours his internal organs and kills him.

Ryan Reynolds plays the role of Rory Adams, a USA ISS engineer. The film is a sci-fi horror genre. It was well-received and grossed a total of $100.5 million at the box office. Reviews mention that the film is well-acted and thrilling. The film was nominated for best science film at the 44th Saturn Awards.

In 2017, he got a star in the Hollywood Hall of Fame.

In 2018, a sequel to *Deadpool* was released, and it became the highest-grossing movie of all time until *Joker* was released in 2019.

He appeared in *6 Underground* as a wealthy man who faked his death to fight crime. The film was critically acclaimed.

He also was the voice of Detective Pikachu in the *Pokemon: Pikachu* film that was released in 2019.

2020 came and with the pandemic. Ryan Reynolds announced that he was returning to *The Croods* as the voice of the guy. He became the executive producer of the ABC game show *Don't*.

In 2021, Ryan came back to play the role of Michael Bryce in the sequel to *The Hitman's Bodyguard*. This one is titled *The Hitman's Wife's Bodyguard*. In this installment, Darius Kincaid's wife, Sonia, tracks down Bryce while he's preparing to retire and go on a vacation. She enlists him to help her rescue her husband, who has been kidnapped by mobsters. On their way, they are met by an Interpol agent who needs their help to catch a terrorist, Aristotle, who wants to destroy the European power grid because Europe wants to impose strict sanctions on Greece.

Aristotle attacks them, Bryce is injured, and enlists help from his stepfather, Bryce senior. Aristotle kidnaps them; he is able to escape, leaving Sonia, who has a past with Aristotle. He rescues Kincaid, and they go to rescue Sonia. He finds out Bryce senior is working for Aristotle. They rescue Sonia, and he is able to override Aristotle's plan to destroy the power grid. He signs papers allowing the Kincaids to adopt him thinking it was his bodyguard license. Interpol promises to clear them after 48 hours.

He also played the role of Guy in *Free Guy*, a scientific action-comedy. Guy is a bank teller and a monolayer in the free city where their life is determined by the players who play the game in a video game world.

Ryan loved the film and thinks he's lucky to be part of such a great film. For Ryan, it was an exhilarating experience. He was part of the screenwriting, production, and marketing. He mentioned that these days, most films are sequels or based on a comic book. The characters are already known. It was a big deal for him to be part of a new project, giving life to something new. Ryan loved playing the character of Guy. He said, "There's something wonderful playing Guy, who is like a four year old adult." The character of Guy is innocent and sweetly naive, something different from what we're used to from Ryan Reynolds. The film was well-received. It made a box office total of $331.5 million. It also won a people's choice award and was nominated for an academy award. Ryan's role of Guy was beautifully played, and he was not left out in awards. He was nominated for two People's Choice Awards and a Kid's Choice Award.

For his last film in 2021, he starred alongside Dwayne Johnson and Gal Gaddot in Netflix's action thriller, *Red Notice*. Viewers loved the film. It was hilarious and well-acted. One can say it was a feel-good film. It was criticized for its lack of originality. There are two sequels in the making.

After the release of *Red Notice*, Ryan announced he was taking a little break from work. He starred in *The Adam Project*, which was released in 2022. The film was well acted and funny. It goes on to prove that Ryan Reynolds is in a class of his own when it comes to acting.

"Deadpool 2 Japan Premiere Red Carpet: Ryan Reynolds" by Dick Thomas Johnson is licensed under CC BY 2.0

Ryan Reynolds' Awards and Achievements

Ryan Reynold has created a quirky and quick-witted persona on TV due to most of his roles played. Currently, he's one of the most popular and well-recognized Canadian actors in the Hollywood industry. He has starred in so many blockbuster movies that it'll be no surprise he has been nominated for various awards at different intervals. Ryan has exhibited great acting skills while acting alongside other actors and actresses, each holding high expectations of him. As he's still currently active in his acting career, there is a greater possibility of him winning many more awards to come.

All of Ryan Reynolds' Nominations for various awards are listed below:

He was nominated for the Critic's Choice Movie Award two times as

- Best Actor in an Action Movie (*Deadpool*) - 2016

- Best Actor in a comedy (*Deadpool*) - 2016

He was nominated for the *Entertainment Weekly* Entertainer of the year Awards as

- Entertainer of the Year - 2016

He was nominated for the Golden Globe Awards once as

- Best Actor- Motion Picture Musical or Comedy (*Deadpool*) - 2017

He was nominated for the Gotham Awards once as

- Best Ensemble Cast (*Adventure Land*) -2009

He was nominated for the Goya Awards once as

- Best Actor (*Buried*) - 2010

He was nominated for the MTV Awards ten times as

- Breakthrough Male Performance (*Van Wilder*) - 2003

- Best Comedic Performance (*The Proposal*) - 2010

- Best Kiss (*The Proposal*) -2010

- Best Fight (*X-Men Origin: Wolverine*) - 2010

- Best Scared as shit Performance (*Buried*) - 2011

- Best Male Performance (*Deadpool*) -2016

- Best Action Performance (*Deadpool*) - 2016

- Best Kiss (*Deadpool*) - 2016

- Best Comedic Performance (*Deadpool*) - 2016

- Best Fight (*Deadpool*) -2016

He was nominated for the Grammy Awards once for

- Best Compilation Soundtrack for Visual Media (*Deadpool*)- 2019

He was nominated for the Nickelodeon Kids Choice Awards two times

- Favorite Voice from an animated movie (*The Croods: A New Age*)- 2021

- Favorite Movie Actor (*Free Guy* and *Red Notice*) - 2022

He was nominated for the People's Choice Awards thirteen times as

- Favorite Comedy Star (*The Proposal*) - 2010

- Favorite Movie Actor (*The Proposal*) - 2010

- Favorite On-screen team (*The Proposal* and *X-Men Origin: Wolverine*) - 2010

- Favorite Movie Superhero (*Green Lantern*) - 2012

- Favorite Action Movie Star (*Green Lantern*) - 2012

- Favorite Comedic Movie Star (*The Change-Up*) - 2012

- Favorite Movie Actor (*Green Lantern*) - 2012

- Favorite Movie Actor (*Deadpool*) - 2017

- Favorite Action Movie Actor (*Deadpool*) - 2017

- The Action Movie Star of 2018 (*Deadpool*) - 2018

- The Male Movie Star of 2021 (*Free Guy*) - 2021

- The Comedy Movie Star of 2021 (*Free Guy*) - 2021

He was nominated for the Producers Guild of America once for

- Best Theatrical Motion Picture (*Deadpool*) - 2017

He was nominated for the San Diego Film Critics Society Awards once for

- Best Comedic Performance (*Deadpool*) - 2016

He was nominated for the Saturn Awards two times as

- Best Actor (*Buried*) - 2011

- Best Actor (*Deadpool*) - 2017

He was nominated for the Teen Choice Awards nine times for

- Choice Movie Scary Scene (*The Amityville Horror*) - 2005

- Choice Summer Movie Star (*The Proposal*) - 2009

- Choice Movie Actor: Romantic Comedy (*The Proposal*) - 2010

- Choice Movie: Chemistry (*The Proposal*) - 2010

- Choice Movie: Liplock (*The Proposal*) -2010

- Choice Movie Actor: Sci-Fi/Fantasy (*Green Lantern*) - 2011

- Choice Movie Actor: Action (*Deadpool*) - 2016

- Choice Movie: Hissy Fit (*Deadpool*) - 2016

- Choice Comedy Movie Actor (*Pokemon Detective Pikachu*) - 2019

He was nominated for the Miscellaneous Awards four for

- Young Artist Awards (Best Young Actor Co-Starring in a Cable Series) - 1993

- Young Hollywood Awards (Next-Generation Male) - 2003

- Hasty Pudding's Man of the Year (Man of the Year) - 2017

- Governor General's Performing Arts Awards - 2021

From the above, one can see that Ryan Reynolds has received a total of 49 nominations for various awards, of which he has won a total of 13.

His Critic's Choice Movie Awards include

- Best Actor in Comedy (*Deadpool*) - Year 2016

Ryan Reynolds 2016 Critic's Choice Best Actor in a Comedy

http://allaboutbookseries.com/CriticsChoiceBestActorComedy2016

His *Entertainment Weekly* Entertainer of the Year Award includes;

- Entertainer of the Year - Year 2016

Ryan Reynolds 2016 Entertainer of the Year

http://allaboutbookseries.com/EntertaineroftheYear2016

His MTV Movie Awards include

- Best Comedic Performance (*Deadpool*) - Year 2016

- Best Fight (*Deadpool*) - Year 2016

His People's Choice Award includes

- Favorite Movie Superhero (*Green Lantern*) - Year 2012

- Favorite Action Movie Star (*Green Lantern*) - Year 2012

- Favorite Movie Actor (*Deadpool*) - Year 2017

His Saturn Award includes

- Best Actor (*Deadpool*) - Year 2017

His Teen Choice Awards include

- Choice Movie Scary Scene (*The Amityville Horror*) - Year 2005

- Choice Movie: Hissy Fit (*Deadpool*) - Year 2016

Innovator Award, *WSJ Magazine* (2021)

His Miscellaneous Awards include

- Young Hollywood Awards as Next Generation Male - Year 2003

- Hasty Pudding's Man of the Year as Man of the Year - Year 2017

- Governor General's Performing Arts Awards. He won the National Arts Centre Award - Year 2021

His Other Achievements

When you hear Ryan Reynolds, you instantly think of *Deadpool*. This is a result of the massive success the hit movie gathered. However, other than his notable characters in movies, Ryan has a few other achievements. On the Hollywood Walk of Fame, he was inducted in 2017 for the category of Motion Pictures. He also has a star on Canada's Walk of Fame. In 2010, he was named the Sexiest Man Alive by *People Magazine* after appearing on the list twice in 2007 and 2009, respectively. Ryan is also a member of the board of directors of the Michael Fox Foundation. To show he's a king of duality, Ryan showed his singing skills when he performed "Tomorrow" on May 13, 2018. He did this in the opening show of the South Korean reality TV show, *King of Masked Singer.*

Ryan Reynolds Works Outside Acting

Sometime around January 2018, Ryan Reynolds began his own production company called Maximum Effort, after which he signed a contract with Fox for three years. You can call him the backbone of this production company as he has worked hard to advertise most of the movie projects he participated in. He also offered adverts for a few other brands like R.M. Williams and Peloton.

In that same year, around February, Ryan Reynolds purchased a share in Aviation American Gin. He had stated that he had an interest in this business, especially the product. He declared his intention to be active in this area. Ryan doesn't stop there as he's quite interested in business, so in 2019, particularly in November, he goes on to purchase a share in Mint Mobile. Reports later showed that Ryan owned about 20-25% of Mint Mobile.

In July 2020, Ryan took a step forward by becoming a member of the Board of Match Group, an online technology company that offers online dating services. On September 23, 2020, Ryan was rumored to be participating in a business partnership alongside fellow actor Rob McElhenney, which was later confirmed by the Wrexham Supporters Trust. The purpose of the partnership talks was to acquire the Wrexham AFC, a Welsh football club. On November 16, the news became official that Ryan had taken over the club. Ryan was quite smart enough to use his takeover of the Welsh football club to publicize his Netflix movie, *Red Notice*, which he did alongside Dwayne Johnson.

Ryan Reynolds Charity and Advocacy Work

Over the years, Ryan has been well known to be an activist and environmentalist. Back in 2008, it was discovered that he had participated in the New York City Marathon just to be able to gather money to donate to the Michael Fox Foundation. This was to honor his dead father, who suffered from Parkinson's disease. It was also noted that Ryan had teamed up with the environmental organization Natural Resources Defense Group to show his support for renewable energy and also increase awareness of the effects of oil leakage in the Mexico water areas. Ryan is also said to provide support to the Vancouver Covenant's House. This house offers shelter to homeless people. He also supports an institution in Uganda that provides education to children of former soldiers. In 2010, reports stated that Ryan had made an appearance in the concert Canada for Haiti in order to help raise funds following the damage caused by an earthquake in Haiti.

Ryan Reynolds: We've Got To Do All We Can

http://allaboutbookseries.com/WeGotToDoWhatWeCan

Ryan Reynolds' Timeline

October 23, 1976 - Ryan Reynolds was born in Vancouver, British Columbia, Canada

1991 - Ryan Reynolds' acting career commenced with a role in the teen drama Hillside. He was just fifteen at this time.

1993 - He played the role of Ganesh, an Indian, in the movie *Ordinary Magic*. Ryan Reynolds was seventeen years old when he played this role. He was also nominated for the Young Artist Awards as Best young actor co-starring in a cable series. This series was titled Hillside.

1993 and 1994 - He played the recurring role of Marco in the movie *The Odyssey*.

1996 - He appeared in the movie *Sabrina the Teenage Witch* alongside Melissa Joan Hart.

1997 - Ryan played the character Howard in the comedy movie *Life During Wartime*.

1998 - He took on the role of a medical student, Micheal Bergen, in the comical movie *Two Guys, a Girl, and a Pizza Place*.

1999 - He starred in two films. He played the role of Chip Halderman in *Dick* and Henry Rockefeller in *Coming Soon.*

2000 - He starred in the following movies: *Big Monster on Campus*, *We All Fall Down*, and *Buying the Cow.*

2002 - He played the lead role of Van Wilder in the first of the film series *National Lampoon Van Wilder*. This was his breakout role as it got nominated for MTV Awards.

2003 - Ryan took on the role of Kevin in the comedy movie *Foolproof*. He also starred in *Harold and Kumar Go to White Castle* as an OR nurse in the hospital where the main character's brother and father work. This same year, Ryan was nominated for an MTV Movie Award in the category of Breakthrough Male Performance. This was for his role in the movie *Van Wilder*. He also received the Young Hollywood Award as the Next Generation Male.

2004 - He was cast by David Goyer in the last of the Blade Trilogy; *Blade: Trinity.*

2005 - Ryan decided to try a new genre. He was cast as the lead character, George Lutz, in the horror movie *Amityville Horror*. That same year, he was nominated for the Teen's Choice Award under the category of Choice Movie Scary Scene. It was a great feat that he won the award, as that was another stepping block in his career. Ryan also agreed to star in the comedy sports movie *School of Life*, romantic-comedy movie *Just Friends*, and the comedy-indie film *Waiting*.

2006 - He was cast in the action/crime movie *Smokin Aces* as an FBI agent.

2008 - Ryan was cast for the movie *Chaos Theory* where he played the role of Frank Allen. He also starred in the romantic comedy film *Definitely Maybe*, in which he acted alongside Elizabeth Banks. Ryan also got married to the well-renowned actress Scarlett Johansson though the two divorced in 2011.

2009 - He was cast as Wade Wilson in the action-adventure movie *X-men Origins: Wolverine*. Though he didn't play the lead role, Ryan co-starred in the romantic comedy movie *Adventureland*. That same year, the movie was also nominated for the Gotham Award under the category of Best Ensemble Cast. A great year for Ryan Reynolds as he also decided to play the role of Andrew Paxton in the romantic comedy movie *The Proposal* alongside the popular actress Sandra Bullock. The movie was nominated for the Teen's Choice Award for Choice Summer Movie Star.

2010 - Ryan was named the sexiest man alive in *People Magazine*. He took on more serious roles starting with playing Paul Conroy, an American truck driver, in the thriller drama *Buried*. This year, Ryan was nominated for quite a number of awards. He was nominated for the Goya Awards for Best Actor for his movie Buried. He was nominated for the MTV Awards for Best Comedic Performance and Best Kiss in *The Proposal* and Best Fight in *X-Men Origin: Wolverine*. He was also nominated three times for the Teen's Choice Awards for his movie *The Proposal*. Ryan was also nominated for the People's Choice Awards three times for his movies *The Proposal* and *X-Men Origins: Wolverine*.

2011 - Ryan goes on to play the role of a superhero in the DC movie *Green Lantern*. He also stars as Mitch Planko in the movie *The Change-Up*. He was nominated for the Teen's Choice Awards for Choice Movie Actor: Sci-Fi/Fantasy for his movie *Green Lantern*. He was also nominated for the MTV Awards for Best Scared as Shit performance for his thriller drama *Buried*. He was also nominated for Saturn Award and worked on the Canadian documentary, *The Whale*.

2012 - He starred in the action movie *Safe House*. He also appeared in the popular Marvel series *The Avengers*. Ryan was nominated for the People's Choice Awards, three for his movie *Green Lantern* and one for the movie, *The Change-Up*. Lucky enough, he won two of the awards. He also married Blake Lively.

2013 - He played a voice actor for the character Turbo in the animated movie *Turbo*. He also played the voice of a character in the popular animation movie *The Croods*.

2014 - He starred in the action/thriller movie *The Captive* as Matthew. Ryan also goes on to play the role of Jerry Hickfan in the horror/thriller movie *The Voices*. He also appeared in the western/comedy-drama, *A Million Ways to Die in the West*.

2015 - Ryan plays the character Curtis in the indie film *Mississippi Grind*. He also plays the lead role in the sci-fi/action movie *Selfless*. Ryan also starred as Randol in the biographical film *Woman in Gold*.

2016 - Ryan plays his dream role as Wade Wilson in the popular action-adventure movie *Deadpool*. The movie earned him the most awards and nominations in his entire career. He was nominated for the Critic's Choice Movie Awards, *Entertainment Weekly* Entertainer of the Year Awards, MTV Awards, San Diego Film Critics Society Awards, and Teens Choice Awards. He won the Best Actor in Comedy award, Entertainer of the Year Award, Best Fight award, and Best Comedic Performance Award. He also won a Teen's Choice Award. He plays Bill Pope in the action movie *Criminal*.

2017 - Ryan Reynolds plays Rory Adams in the sci-fi *Life*. He also starred alongside Samuel L. Jackson in the movie *The Hitman's Bodyguard*. He won a Hasty Pudding's Man of the Year Award, Saturn Award, People's Choice Awards and was also inducted into the Hollywood Walk of Fame. He was also nominated for the Producers Guild of America Award.

2018 - Ryan plays Wade Wilson in the sequel *Deadpool 2*. He was also nominated for the People's Choice Awards. Ryan began his production company Maximum Effort and also purchased a share of Aviation American Gin.

2019 - Ryan starred as Victor in the franchise *Fast and Furious: Hobbs and Shaw*. He also takes on the role of one in the action film *6 Underground*. He voices Detective Pikachu in the adventure animation *Pokemon Detective Pikachu*, for which he was nominated for the Teen's Choice Awards. He was also nominated for a Grammy Award. Ryan purchased a share of Mint Mobile.

2020 - He voices the character, Guy, in the animation *The Croods 2: New Age*. He became a member of the board of Match Group and also acquired the Wrexham football club.

2021 - He's cast in three movies: *The Hitman's Wife's Bodyguard, Red Notice*, and *Free Guy*. Ryan won the Governor General's Performing Arts Awards, and was nominated for the Nickelodeon Kids Choice Awards and People's Choice Awards.

2022 - Ryan played Adam Reed in the sci-fi movie *The Adam Project*. He was nominated for the Nickelodeon Kids Choice Awards for his movies *Free Guy* and *Red Notice*.

Final Surprise Bonus

Hope you've enjoyed this biography of Ryan Reynolds.

We always like to give more than we get, so I'd like to give you one final bonus.

Do me a favor, if you enjoyed this book, *please* leave a review on Amazon.

It'll help get the word out so more kids can find out more about Ryan Reynolds!

If you do, I'll send you one of my most cherished video collection – Free:

Ultimate Collection of Links to Ryan Reynolds' YouTube Videos!

You won't be able to say you know Ryan Reynolds until you watch these videos!

Here's how to claim your free videos:

1. Leave a review right away -

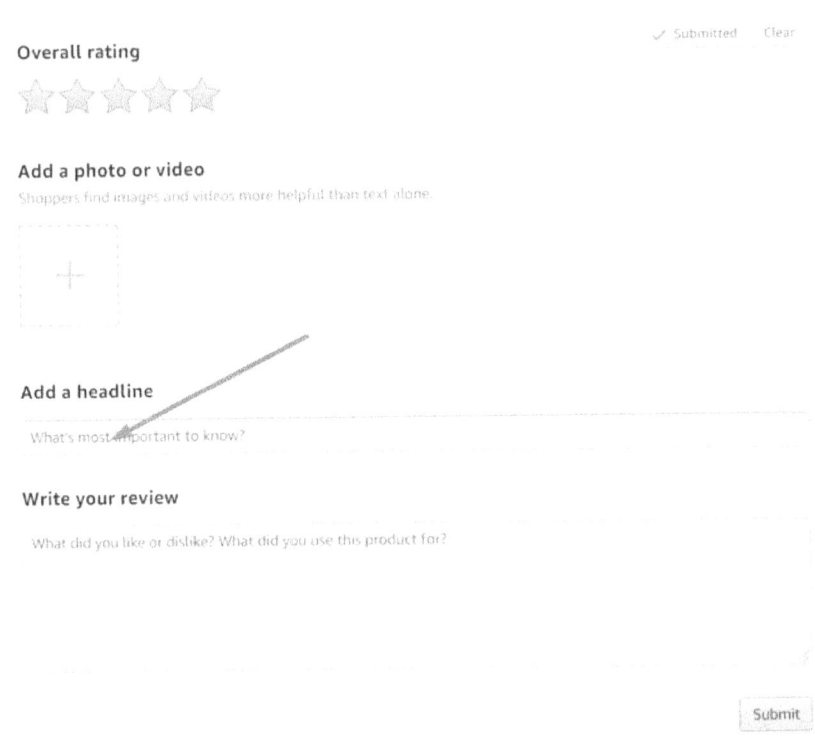

2. Send a screenshot of your review to: reviews@allaboutbookseries.com with the subject line: All About Ryan Reynolds Review

3. Receive your free video collection – "Ultimate Collection of Links to Ryan Reynolds' YouTube Videos! " – *immediately*!